Smithsonian

LITTLE EXPLORER

The U.S. Constitution

Introducing Primary Sources

by Kathryn Clay

CAPSTONE PRESS
a capstone imprint

Little Explorer is published by Capstone Press,
1710 Roe Crest Drive, North Mankato, Minnesota 56003
www.mycapstone.com

Library of Congress Cataloging-in-Publication Data
Clay, Kathryn, author.
The U.S. Constitution : introducing primary sources / by Kathryn Clay.
pages cm. — (Smithsonian little explorer. introducing primary sources.)
Includes bibliographical references and index.
Summary: "Introduces young readers to primary sources related to the U.S. constitution"— Provided
by publisher.
ISBN 978-1-4914-8225-4 (library binding)
ISBN 978-1-4914-8609-2 (paperback)
ISBN 978-1-4914-8615-3 (eBook PDF)
1. Constitutional history—United States—Juvenile literature. 2. United States. Constitution—Juvenile
literature. I. Title.
KF4541.C53 2016
342.7302′4—dc23   2015030752

Editorial Credits
Michelle Hasselius, editor; Richard Parker, designer; Wanda Winch, media researcher;
Steve Walker, production specialist

Our very special thanks to Jennifer L. Jones, Chair, Armed Forces Division at the National Museum
of American History, Kenneth E. Behring Center, Smithsonian, for her curatorial review. Capstone
would also like to thank Kealy Gordon, Product Development Manager, and the following at
Smithsonian Enterprises: Ellen Nanney, Licensing Manager; Brigid Ferraro, Vice President, Education
and Consumer Products; Carol LeBlanc, Senior Vice President, Education and Consumer Products.

Photo Credits
Bridgeman Images: Bequest of Miss Helen C. Banning 1913/Art Gallery of New South Wales, Sydney,
Australia/William Owen, 15; Corbis: Demotix/Alex Neely, 27; Dreamstime: Americanspirit, 26; From
the Lincoln Financial Foundation Collection, courtesy of the Indiana State Museum and Allen County
Public Library, 23 (top); Granger, NYC, 8 (right), 9 (right), 11 (top), 21 (top); Library of Congress: Prints
and Photographs Division, 11 (bottom), 17 (top), 23 (bottom), 24, 25, 28, 29, The George Washington
Papers 1741–1799, 7 (left), Manuscript Division/William Paterson Papers, 14, Broadsides, leaflets, and
pamphlets from America and Europe, 8 (left), 19, 20, 21 (bottom), Manuscript Division/James Madison
Papers, 10, 18 (right), Manuscript Division/Thomas Jefferson Papers, 22; National Archives and
Records Administration, 7 (right), ourdocuments.gov/Articles of Confederation, 6, ourdocuments.gov/
U.S. Constitution, 5, ourdocuments.gov/Virginia Plan, 12; Shutterstock: Onur Ersin, cover, Robynrg,
18 (left); White Historic Art: Bryant White, 9 (left); White House Historical Association (White House
Collection), 4; Wikimedia, 16; Yale University Art Gallery, 13

Printed in the United States of America in North Mankato, Minnesota.
009221CGS16

Table of Contents

Primary Sources

What is a primary source? A primary source is created during an event. It could be a photo, a painting, a letter, or a newspaper article. People can use primary sources to learn about history. The U.S. Constitution is a primary source. Other primary sources include the U.S. flag and the Liberty Bell.

a painting from 1873 of founding fathers signing the Declaration of Independence

Citizens in the United States are protected by a group of laws. The laws explain what we can and cannot do. These laws are known as the U.S. Constitution.

The U.S. Constitution at a Glance

- written in 1787
- signed in Philadelphia, Pennsylvania
- signed by 39 men, including George Washington, Benjamin Franklin, and James Madison
- 4,400 words long
- displayed at the National Archives in Washington, D.C.

Articles of Confederation

The United States started as 13 colonies. Each colony had its own laws. They sent leaders to the Continental Congress. The Continental Congress made laws for the whole country.

the Articles of Confederation, written in 1777

> *"... a half-starved limping government, that appears to be always moving upon the crutches and tottering at every step."*
>
> —letter from George Washington to Benjamin Harrison

Washington's letter to Benjamin Harrison about coming together as a nation and having a strong federal government

Leaders wrote the first set of laws in 1777. The Continental Congress called them the Articles of Confederation. Members of Congress were careful not to make too many rules.

Colonists did not want the government to have too much power. They feared the U.S. government would become too similar to Britain's rule. To protest many people did not follow the laws.

a drawing of colonists in the late 1700s

Shays' Rebellion

After the Revolutionary War (1775–1783), America became its own country. The colonies eventually became states. To support the growing country, America needed money. The only way to get it was to tax every citizen.

In this painting from 1786, a blacksmith is taxed during Shays' Rebellion.

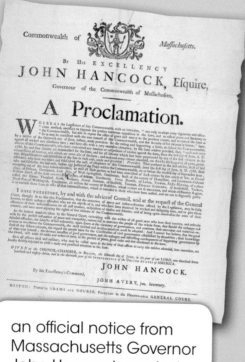

an official notice from Massachusetts Governor John Hancock against Shays' Rebellion in 1787

Massachusetts raised taxes on farmland. Many colonists couldn't pay the taxes and were arrested. People like Daniel Shays grew angry. Shays gathered more than 1,000 colonists to protest the taxes. In 1787 the protesters attacked the place where federal weapons were stored in Springfield, Massachusetts.

a painting from 1787 of the Shays' Rebellion attack in Springfield

Government leaders knew something had to change. The country needed laws that everyone would follow.

FACT

Daniel Shays was a captain in the Continental army during the Revolutionary War.

Constitutional Convention

The Constitutional Convention was held in May 1787. Twelve of the 13 states sent people to speak. This group became known as the founding fathers.

James Madison's notes during the convention in 1787

FACT

Rhode Island did not send a representative to the Constitutional Convention. Rhode Island wanted the government to stay the same.

The group met for four months. They decided how to create new laws. They also wanted each state to have its own power.

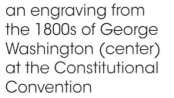

an engraving from the 1800s of George Washington (center) at the Constitutional Convention

The Founding Fathers

A total of 55 founding fathers attended the convention. Many were lawyers. Some were teachers, farmers, or doctors. Benjamin Franklin was the oldest founding father. He was 81. Other founding fathers included George Washington and James Madison.

Benjamin Franklin in 1780

Dividing Power

The founding fathers wanted to split up the government's power. No one group would have complete control. James Madison suggested three branches. The legislative branch would make laws. The executive branch would make sure the laws were followed. The judicial branch would explain the laws. This idea was called the Virginia Plan.

the Virginia Plan, written by James Madison in 1787

> *"The question is, not what rights naturally belong to man, but how they may be most equally and effectually guarded in society."*
>
> —Roger Sherman

Roger Sherman

Connecticut representative Roger Sherman was also one of the founding fathers. He suggested that the legislative branch be made up of the Senate and House of Representatives.

Sherman was the only person to sign all four documents of the American Revolution. These documents included the Continental Association of 1774, the Declaration of Independence, the Articles of Confederation, and the U.S. Constitution.

13

William Paterson's notes from 1787 about his plan, the New Jersey Plan

In the Virginia Plan, the number of representatives for each state was based on how many people lived there. That meant larger states would have more power. Smaller states did not like this plan.

William Paterson of New Jersey suggested a new idea. He said each state should send one person. This idea was called the New Jersey Plan. Larger states voted for the Virginia Plan. Smaller states voted for the New Jersey Plan.

a portrait of William Paterson in 1799

The Great Compromise

Roger Sherman suggested a compromise. Each state would have two members in the Senate. The House of Representatives would be different. States with more people would have more members.

a draft of Sherman's Great Compromise, also known as the Connecticut Compromise

a cartoon published in 1787 about political issues in Connecticut during the time the U.S. Constitution was written

Southern states wanted slaves counted as part of their population. Then these states would have more members in the House of Representatives. Northern states did not like this idea. They were against slavery.

FACT

The states later agreed slaves would be counted. For every 100 slaves, the southern states could count 60 toward their population.

Signing the Constitution

The first draft of the Constitution was completed on August 6, 1787. Not everyone was happy. Some of the founding fathers wanted a bill of rights. This would protect individual rights, including freedom of speech and religion. Others argued it wasn't needed. States already had their own bill of rights.

the back the $2 bill shows members of the Continental Congress

a proposed bill of rights that was rejected at the Constitutional Convention in 1787

The final draft was completed five weeks later. It did not have a bill of rights. On September 17, 1787, 39 of the 55 founding fathers signed the U.S. Constitution.

a painting from 1925 of founding fathers signing the U.S. Constitution

Newspapers in each state printed the Constitution. People who agreed with the Constitution were called Federalists. Those who disagreed called themselves Anti-Federalists.

wood carving from 1890 of colonists reading in a New York coffeehouse

State of Rhode-Island and Providence-Plantations.

In GENERAL ASSEMBLY.

January Session, A.D. 1790.

An ACT for calling a CONVENTION, to take into Consideration the Constitution proposed for the United States, passed on the 17th of September, A.D. 1787, by the GENERAL CONVENTION held at Philadelphia.

BE it Enacted by this General Assembly, and by the Authority thereof it is hereby Enacted, That the New Constitution proposed for the United States, passed on the 17th of September, A.D. 1787, by the GENERAL CONVENTION held at Philadelphia, be submitted to the People of this State, represented in a STATE CONVENTION, for their full and free Investigation and Decision, agreeably to the Resolve of the said Convention: That it be recommended to the Freemen of the several Towns, qualified to vote in the Election of Deputies to the General Assembly, to convene in their respective Town, in legal Town-Meeting, on the Second Monday in February next; and then to choose the same Number of Delegates as they are entitled to elect Deputies, to represent them in the said Convention: And that the said Convention be holden at South-Kingstown, on the First Monday in March next.

And be it further Enacted by the Authority aforesaid, That the said Convention be and hereby is empowered, and fully authorized, finally to decide on the said Constitution, as they shall judge to be most conducive to the Interests of the People of this State: And that the said Convention cause the Result of their Deliberations and Proceedings, relative to the aforesaid Constitution, to be transmitted to the PRESIDENT of the United States of America, as soon after the Rising thereof as may be.

It is Voted and Resolved, That his Excellency the Governor be and he is hereby requested, to transmit a Copy of this Act to the President of the said United States immediately.

It is Ordered, That the Secretary cause Copies hereof to be transmitted to each Town-Clerk in the State, without the least Delay.

A true Copy:

Witness, HENRY WARD, Se'ry.

FACT
Rhode Island was the 13th state to ratify the U.S. Constitution.

a notice for an official meeting in Rhode Island to discuss the proposed U.S. Constitution

The Constitution was not law yet. Nine out of the 13 states needed to ratify it. Federalists worked hard to change minds. They said the Constitution could be changed at a later date.

On June 21, 1788, the ninth state accepted the U.S. Constitution. It became law. All 13 states eventually ratified the Constitution.

newspaper article published in 1788 announcing the ratification of the U.S. Constitution

SUPPLEMENT
TO THE
Independent Journal,
New-York, July 2, 1788.

In our Independent Journal of this Morning, we announced the Ratification of the New Constitution by the Convention of Virginia: For the gratification of our Readers, we publish the following particulars, received by this day's post:—

Ratification of the New Constitution, by the Convention of Virginia, on Wednesday last, by a Majority of 10:---88 for it, 78 against it.

WE the delegates of the people of Virginia, duly elected, in pursuance of a recommendation of the General Assembly, and now met in Convention, having fully and fairly investigated and discussed the proceedings of the Federal Convention, and being prepared as well as the most mature deliberation will enable us to decide thereon, DO, in the name and on behalf of the people of Virginia, declare and make known, that the powers granted under the Constitution being derived from the people of the ... ates, may be resumed ... whensoever the same ... verted to their in ... oppression, and that every power not granted there by remains with them, and at

With these impressions, with a solemn appeal to the searcher of hearts for the purity of our intentions, and under the conviction, that whatsoever imperfections may exist in the Constitution, ought rather to be examined in the mode prescribed therein, than to bring the UNION into danger by a delay, with a hope of obtaining amendments previous to the ratification:

We the said delegates, in the name and in behalf of the people of Virginia, do by these presents assent to and ratify the Constitution, recommended on the 17th day of September, 1787, by the Federal Convention, for the government of the United States; hereby announcing to all those whom it may concern, that the said

Changing the Constitution

Thomas Jefferson kept a record of the amendments that were ratified.

FACT

Changes to the U.S. Constitution are called amendments. The first 10 amendments that have been ratified make up the Bill of Rights.

Slavery was a major issue during the 1800s. Northern states did not allow people to own slaves. Southern states did. The Civil War (1861–1865) began in part because the states could not agree about slavery.

Harper's Weekly drawing from May 1861 of Civil War soldiers marching off to war

a photo of a farm in Virginia in the 1860s

After years of fighting, the North won the Civil War. The government wanted to protect former slaves. On December 18, 1865, lawmakers approved the 13th Amendment. This ended slavery in the United States.

At first only men were allowed to vote in the United States. Women also wanted a say in government decisions. In the 1880s women fought for the right to vote. They wrote letters. They marched in parades.

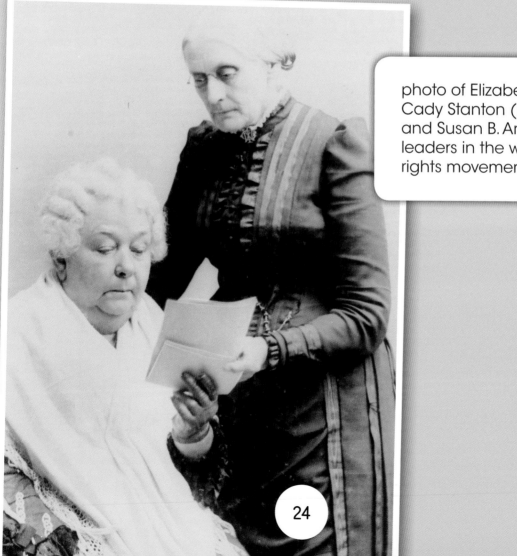

photo of Elizabeth Cady Stanton (seated) and Susan B. Anthony, leaders in the women's rights movement

photos of women marching for the right to vote in Washington, D.C., in 1914

On August 26, 1920, their efforts were rewarded. The 19th Amendment was added to the Constitution. This means that women are allowed to vote in all U.S. elections.

The Constitution Today

In 1787 the U.S. Constitution began with "We the People." These words have never changed. In fact none of the original words have changed. Only amendments have been added.

The U.S. Constitution and Bill of Rights at the National Archives in Washington, D.C.

photo from 2013 of protesters speaking in Washington, D.C.

More than 9,000 amendments have been suggested since 1787. Only 27 have been added to the Constitution so far. These amendments give equal rights to all people. They give freedom of speech and religion. They make sure that the government does not have too much power over its people.

Timeline

a drawing of the Battle of Lexington during the Revolutionary War

1775   the Revolutionary War begins

1777   the first set of U.S. laws, called the Articles of Confederation, are drafted by the Continental Congress

1783   the Revolutionary War ends

1786–1787   Shays' Rebellion takes place

May 1787   the Constitutional Convention begins

August 1787   the first complete draft of the U.S. Constitution is written

June 1788	the U.S. Constitution is ratified and becomes law
1789	the Bill of Rights is written
May 1790	Rhode Island is the last state to ratify the Constitution
December 1791	the Bill of Rights is officially added to the U.S. Constitution
December 1865	the 13th Amendment ending slavery is added to the Constitution
August 1920	the 19th Amendment giving women the right to vote is added to the Constitution

a photo of a woman voting for the first time in Pittsburgh, Pennsylvania

Glossary

Bill of Rights—a list of 10 amendments to the U.S. Constitution that protect your right to speak freely, practice religion, and other important rights

colonist—someone who lives in a newly settled area

compromise—to come to an agreement

convention—a formal meeting

evidence—information and facts that help prove something happened or make you believe something is true

federal—relating to the U.S. government

legislature—a group of people who have the power to make or change laws for a country or state

population—the total number of people who live in a certain place

primary source—an original document

protest—to object to something strongly and publicly

ratify—to officially approve

rebellion—armed fight against a government

slavery—the owning of another person; slaves are forced to work without pay

tax—money that people or businesses must pay to the government

U.S. Congress—the branch of U.S. government that makes laws; Congress is made up of the Senate and the House of Representatives

Read More

Richmond, Benjamin. *What Are the Three Branches of the Government?: And Other Questions About the U.S. Constitution.* Good Question! New York: Sterling Children's Books, 2014.

Slade, Suzanne. *A Bill's Journey into Law.* Mankato, Minn.: Picture Window Books, 2012.

Stier, Catherine. *Today on Election Day.* New York: AV2 by Weigl, 2013.

Internet Sites

FactHound offers a safe, fun way to find Internet sites related to this book. All of the sites on FactHound have been researched by our staff.

Here's all you do:

Visit *www.facthound.com*

Type in this code: 9781491482254

Check out projects, games and lots more at
www.capstonekids.com

Critical Thinking Using the Common Core

1. The Continental Congress wrote the first set of laws for America. What were these laws called? (Key Ideas and Details)

2. What is the difference between federalists and anti-federalists? Use the text to help you with your answer. (Key Ideas and Details)

3. The Bill of Rights is made up of 10 amendments. What is an amendment? (Craft and Structure)

Index